MW00386699

THE CYRENEAN PRAYERS

BY RICHARD M. LUKESH

Cover design by Matthew Lukesh

Copyright © 2008 Richard M. Lukesh
All rights reserved.

ISBN: 1-4392-1057-8
ISBN-13: 9781439210574

Visit www.booksurge.com to order additional copies.

OR
AMAZON.com

DEDICATION

This book is dedicated to my mother and father,
who instilled in me the qualities of love, caring, and giving;
to my beautiful wife, Christine, who has been a beacon of love and hope
throughout thirty-six years of blissful marriage;
to our wonderful children, Matt and Sarah,
who reflect those important characteristics of love, caring, and giving;
and finally, to Father William Scully, OFM, my Prodigal Father,
who welcomed my return with a kiss upon the cheek
and a brush from his unshaven whiskers.

ACKNOWLEDGEMENTS

The Cyrenean Prayers would not have been possible without assistance from above—that is plain and simple. A special thank you to my wife, Christine, who spent endless hours editing and formatting, in addition to questioning, probing, offering suggestions, and just being there for me; for this, I am eternally grateful. To Matt and Sarah for always believing in me, as did my dear parents; and to all those who read selected poems and responded with "goose bumps" to the words, the tone, the meanings. My thanks to you all.

CONTENTS

I

II

I

DIVINE PEACE

I felt my heartbeat pounding,
before my mother knew I was there.
My Father sent me to her with love
to follow His commands of love,
for the love of all.

I remember the jostle of her womb,
cradling me so gently with movements—
singing songs of holiness,
singing songs of hope,
nourishing me with love.

I see my heart with love and pain;
I see my world and future before me.
I know what is to be and to become;
some of which is so pure and beautiful;
some, derision and pain.

I am welcomed to the world
by smiles of joy from my mother,
by hand-strength of my new father,
and by the gentleness of the lamb.
The straw is warm and welcoming.

I crawl among wood chips,
throwing them high in the air,
and laughing and squealing with delight,
only to have my mother sweep me up,
and hold me close to her breast.

I walk and play among the palms
to be cooled and to dream and to pray.

I must heal the pain of the sick and poor,
I must teach the sinner repentance,
and I must gather the souls of the faithful.

In the temple I become angry, and
I thrash out at the money-changers,
scattering their sin about the marble floor,
teaching the elders of sins, and
I am ushered homeward by mother.

As I travel in time and age in this world,
my Father's love is growing in me daily;
I answer my mother's bidding at a wedding,
and the wine is replenished lovingly;
my mother's smile is my reward.

I often find myself praying alone; yet I am
healing the sick, erasing the demons, raising the dead.
I bring justice to ravaged women,
I bring hope to the poor and suffering, and
I bring faith to all the downtrodden.

I find myself heralded a King
atop a donkey and with palms sweeping a path,
with throngs of people welcoming me.
The flourish and fanfare bodes not well, and
I feel a warm smile upon my cheek.

My disciples are by my side on this march.
They pave the way before me, and
the cheering roars relentlessly, the voices chant
my coming—yet I sense a darkening about me;
a shadowy, unlit insult about to rear its presence.

We gather in the home of a friend for dinner,
with much lively discussion of the future.
I say to them to break bread and drink wine,
to believe in this as my body and blood, for
the future of the world is in their hands.

And I speak of one who will betray me,
and there is a hushed silence among them.
They question me of his nature, his desires.
I respond that he must do what he does, and
one lurks lonely at the end of the table.

It is time for prayer alone with my Father;
my friends Peter, James, and John join me.
They will stand guard, and I smile, for
I know they will sleep as they shroud me.
The cock crows thrice and I am alone no more.

The torches beam brightly balanced only
by the wrinkle of sword and armor.
The one called Judas comes to me, smiles,
and calls me Master with a kiss on my cheek.
I search his eyes and see only emptiness.

I now face the procurator, Pilate.
He asks me of my crime; I say nothing.
Others shriek *blasphemy, heresy, danger.*
He winces at my innocence, shies away.
Yet the crowd cries *Barabbas!*, and he is free.

I am stripped and tied to a pillar;
the sting of the knot rips open my flesh;
the Roman gurgles and grunts with each lash.
I slump to my knees with each blow,

This pain is only for good.

I am forced to my feet and given a robe;
as I stand, a thorn bites into my forehead, and
a trickle of blood blinds my eyes.
A cross is thrust upon my shoulders, and
I am forced on my journey.

The jeers and spit of the crowd greet me
as I stumble my way on the stones.
I fall a first time from the weight of the cross.
A man from the crowd is forced to assist me;
He is strong and carries the beam.

He does not complain of his service.
His eyes meet mine as we collapse together.
We journey over sand and stone
until we reach the summit; he is released.
I continue my passage alone.

Once again I am stripped of my garments,
pushed down upon my cross, arms stretched outward.
I feel the pain of the nail piercing my flesh,
I feel the pain of the nail on my feet.
I feel my Being hoisted to the heavens.

I sigh and look to my left to see another;
He screams and begs me to save him.
I sigh and look to my right to see another;
he bows his head and asks me to forgive him.
My choice is an easy one.

And at the third hour, my Father takes me.
My lanced side and torn body are all His.

I have completed my work here, and
He knows what I have done—
for Him and for them.

The tears of the women wash me clean.
I am anointed with oils and cleansed again.
I am wrapped in the purest of linen.
As I lie in my tomb I reflect on my life.
On the third day, I am free—again.

J O S E P H

I am but a poor carpenter.
I work at my craft;
I shape wood for use;
I turn dead wood into life,
I turn dead wood into comfort.

I see a young girl, Mary.
She is so beautiful and pure,
and she will be mine to love.
At once, I notice a gift in her eye;
a beam of hope surrounds her.

We marry in joyous occasion, and
our love is so pure and content.
She tells me of a Child soon to bear,
and I know not of what she speaks, yet
I know a joyous feeling.

And when He is born so innocent,
so clean and pure,
I know He is mine.
I know that He must be shared
with all.

He is such a rapture, and
He plays in my shop joyfully.
He smiles at all that I do, and
I smile at Him at every moment.
We are such good friends.

And then He travels away from me,
with His thoughts and actions.
He has other journeys to travel,
other roads to share.
And I miss Him already.

DESERT PRINCE

I came forth from a barren womb,
and now I walk amidst barren lands;
I am the son of disbelief.
A tunic of camel's hair scars my skin
with each trudge of step through desert sand.
I preach to those who thirst for truth;
my words are those of a simple man.
I come to lead the way for a greater one; and
one day He stands before me in the water.
He knows what I must do; I know what I must do;
yet I tremble as the cool water washes His brow,
as each droplet shines with greatness—
I have now become His humble servant.
And at once, my words possess pure meaning:
Above wealth and power, all is His.
The words emptied from my soul:
Behold the Lamb of God, the true one
Who washes away all guilt and sin.
One who provides warmth for the poor;
One Whose sandal I am not worthy to untie.
The purity of the water and the fire of the word
pronounce our eternal salvation.
And yet I continue to feel the pain of injustice;
I proceed to witness the evils of moral decay; and
I will battle them until my head becomes a trophy.
I hear dancing in the distance.

MARY

I am a woman of few words, and
at times I question, *why me?*
I was poor, yet I was wealthy;
I was sad, yet, I was happy.
I do not know why I was called.

An angel of brightness came to me,
told me of my purpose; and
I was awed.
I was alarmed.
I was glorified.

I gave birth in a stable,
I was frightened and cold,
but His warmth was evident,
His joy was immense,
His smile was peace.

We named him Jesus, and
He was a Jesus,
a Jesus smile, a Jesus boy,
a wonderful smile graced
with a silent grace.

And as He grew I saw signs
of His love, of His being;
His patience and calm
His piercing eye when He spoke,
His smile of happiness.

I remember a wedding, a grand affair,
all the family were there, happiness bloomed.

My cousin secretly came to me, chagrined;
the wine was wanting; what to do?
I asked my son to help.

He was not ready, He said.
I told the servants, *Do what He says.*
And when the vessels were filled with water,
the wine became the best.
This was His first. For me.

And one night He said to me:
Mother, I must do what I must do,
please bear with me.
Please let me be.
Do not be afraid.

I then understood what He meant,
but I've never felt so much pain as when
I saw.
No mother should endure
what I endured.

My child, my baby beaten,
by thrashes of cane and whip,
blood sores gaping to the world;
thorns pressed into His brow,
and groans of pain resounding.

I follow His journey
behind crowds of smell and yell,
I see Him fall with the cross,
I see a helper from afar,
I see a veil with His impression.

I am blinded with pain,
I cannot absorb my sight,
I am numb with dumbness,
and I deafen my ears to His anguish,
so much that I faint.

And on that lonely hill,
atop a stony crag of mountain,
He bravely stands mounted
on His symbol.
Forever a memory.

And when it is over,
I cradle Him in my arms,
as I did long ago; only
to gently pull the thorns away,
and feel His soft shoulder upon my breast.

When He is cleaned and spiced
and laid to rest, I only ponder:
no mother should do this,
no mother should suffer so; yet
His peace is my peace.

And on the third day, I visit
to witness an empty tomb.
A feeling of calm surrounds all,
and I know now the reason.
Now, I can smile.

THE COMPASS

I am told that I am a rock,
yet I feel like a mere pebble.
My mouth sprouts words quickly
Well in advance of my thought.
My might and force strike blindly
Thrashing about, wickedly mindless.

He called me to Him upon the water;
I feared for a moment to move but did so.
He called me to pray and guard;
I fell asleep in hidden thought.
He gazed into my eyes and spoke of betrayal;
I denied His words violently.

He called upon me to be His rock;
I said to Him I was not worthy.
He offered me keys to His Kingdom;
I refused; I was not deserving.
He questioned my constant denial of Him;
I lowered my head and wept.

When He left, I felt an emptiness;
I promised myself to hold the keys.
I promised never to deny or betray again;
I would be a compass to guide all—
A compass must be honest and contrite;
A compass must never waver from the Truth.

I, JOHN

His voice brought magic to my eyes;
His eyes sang songs to my ears;
His heart captured my soul, and
His touch warmed my heart;
His peace wrapped me in His warmth.

I remember, once, a quiet moment when
He said to me: *John, love is all.*
Without love, the world is the driest desert.
We must move all to forward the strength,
For love slakes the driest of thirsts.

I remember asking how to do this, and
with the most gentle voice and eye,
He said: *Put your eye in your heart,*
For when your heart sees the pain,
Your heart will soothe the wound.

His hope and faith consoled me.
His absence from the tomb blinded me.
His spirit loomed about and everywhere;
His aura comforted me again, and
His loyal soul guarded my life.

I grasp His peace in my heart,
And in my eye—forever.

CENTURION

I am a man of power;
I command one hundred soldiers.
I say to one: *Go,* and he goes;
I say to another: *Come,* and he comes.
I say to my slave: *Do this,* and it is done.

Yet on this day I am saddened—
my loyal servant lies ill;
he is paralyzed and does not move.
He is the most loyal of servants;
he does my bidding as if it were his own.

No medicine provides a cure;
all prayers go unanswered.
Cold cloths bring no relief.
Wine releases no pain.
He merely stares to the heavens.

I must act and take force;
I must find a permanent cure.
I must be faithful to him, for he
has been devoted to me.
I must resolve his pain.

In Capernaum I hear of a man
who works miracles, a teacher.
I find his location and there is a crowd.
I push forward blindly into the masses;
I look into his eyes for confirmation.

I state the condition of my servant,
of his pain in this world, and he quickly

responds: *Take me to him to be cured.*
He does not know of me, yet
He extends his hand and support.

I am humbled by his presence, and
I respond:
Lord, I am not worthy to have you enter under my roof;
only say the Word and my servant shall be healed.
He looks at me so lovingly.

And then he speaks to me and the crowd:
Many have not believed, but not you.
Go forward, your servant is healed.
Let it be done for you, for you believe.

At my door, my servant greets me.

ROADSIDE

I walk alone, humbly, on the road;
My thoughts drift to my future.
In a dash of light, I am on the earth.
The pain of knuckle brunts my face;
My cheek crushed into the sandy stone.

Rips and tears shred my garments,
Punch and kick pummel my body.
My satchels split from gripped hands, and,
Foul-stenched laughter bellows in my ear
As pain wraps my battered body.

I find myself in a ditch by the road;
My bloodied visage masks my suffering.
The trudge of sandal nearby scrapes my ear;
I see a shadow nudge my shape with a staff—
He sniffs me like a dog and moves on.

Time knows no boundaries—pain does;
I lie in comfort dirt with my moan.
Another man walks the road closely, and
He sights me and stops and stares.
He jabs my bloody head and departs.

At last, a traveler stops a serious moment.
He cradles my head to his breast and sways.
He cleans my wounds with water and lifts me up.
He takes me to an inn for wine and bread.
He pays the charge. I am safe. He leaves.

I lie in peace and consolation;
Pain lessens as I question my savior:
Who was he who saved my life?
Who was he who carried me to safety?

Whoever he was, I love him.

BARTIMAEUS

Shards of rock sliced my eyes in a quarry long ago;
a pain still felt, soul-ending nonetheless.
A stumble became my gait, and laughter became a bitter song;
flowers rendered now useless, and mosaics now dead.

Beauty possessed no meaning, as morning was merely night,
and night loomed as merely night.
Darkness lighted my path as sunless windows
laughed at my blindness.

I heard brightness one day:
His words absorbed all the light,
His words fired like fire, and
His words warmed me.

I begged forgiveness and mercy,
I pleaded for light and sight, and
He simply said: *See.*
My eyes were healed.

My eyes turned to His eyes:
my eyes burned with love.
I had never seen such purity, and
I had never seen true love.

I learned to see His words.
I breathed in His love, and
my blackness turned white,
my darkness shouted radiance.

A second time I was blinded,
when I saw Him on the cross—
His love commanded strength,
His love demanded my light.

I prayed for blindness again,
I did not deserve sight-beauty;
yet I was not alone and weak—
I owned no fear, only strength.

On that third day,
my sight was restored again.

A N O T H E R   C A R P E N T E R

My work makes me a carpenter.
I build what I am told;
whatever must be built, I build.
I am a carpenter.
I make joints with wood;
I join beams together.
I build with wood for a purpose.

My life is built upon wood.
I do what I do—for money.
I have a family to feed.
I do what I do—to survive.
I do what I do—to live.

And I specialize in crosses—
they are easy to make.
The Romans crucify men on them;
I make them every week—it is
easy money for me.
Two planks crossed,
cut, sliced, measured, joiced,
—done.

Another man—another cross.
They break the law—I make a cross.
My last job—
my last cross, was different.

The wood seamed itself together,
almost by itself.
I merely cut and shaved;
the dust and scrapings sparkled

as they dropped to the ground.
The cross formed itself.
For Whom was this to be?

And the next day, I knew.
I saw a Man carry my labor.
I saw a man help Him with His labor,
and I then knew this had been my last cross.
I must carry His.

KING-MAKER

My master—a strange one—
arrives late in the day,
orders me to the thorn patch,
the brambled maze of bronzed,
twisted stickers.
His voice smells strange;
his face is adorned with a mocking look.

I am to gather together
gnarled, thorny, twisted vines,
spikes aplenty,
and form a circle,
like a crown,
a crown to fit a man's head.

I do not question—I do—
I slice the fine vine,
the fresh bendable vine, carefully,
for the thorns point sharp,
like a hundred daggers, and
I twist a circle, a crown.

Each thorn, matched to protect
the other,
pricks my tender fingers.
The crown, stained with my blood
sticks to my hands.
Why? Why—I ask,
for what purpose?
Why should I bleed for a command?
I am only a servant.

I present the prize, the duty
to my master;
he is pleased.
He does not question my bloodied hands,
my scalloped fingertips;
he is only pleased. He smiles.

"This," he exclaims, "is for a King!
You will see on the morrow."
He leaves; the stench of his breath
swirls about the room.
His smell of bitterness—
his smell of contempt.

I sense only fear—
and at the break of the day,
I see a Man, circled with calm,
as my master places the crown
upon His head.

My master presses it deeply upon His crown
so the Blood makes a fine dribble, yet
the Man makes no wince—
He does not cry out.
He stands forward.
My God—I think—
I would have screamed with agony—
I would lose all sense.

Who is this Man before me?
And then I ask, who am I?
What have I done?
I only completed a silly task;
I followed an order.

But what have I done?
This Man is so pure.
Why Him?

I am told He is Jesus.
The parade begins; I drop
to my knees.
I do not know what I have done.

He finds me in the crowd.
He looks at me among hundreds;
His eyes stab mine, like
the thousand daggers of His headpiece.
He knows I am the maker.
I am sorry for what I have done;
I only hope He can forgive me.

Yet I see only love in His eyes—
I see no anger for what I have done.
I cry tears of thorn, and
as He turns,
a speck of Blood graces my brow.

I am forgiven.

S W E E T   I R O N

My forge bristles with red coals
so heated by robust vehemence,
bellow-driven heat waters the eye;
the order of today's work is nails—
as many as I can make.

I hate the making of nails;
I despise the time needed to coax
the iron into shape with twisted head,
and narrowed, pointed spine, and
yet, the seven inches of strength is good.

Tong grips tight the molten mass,
unformed 'til I give it life with pounding,
with turning and shaping of the hammer.
When its death turns dark with water sizzle,
a final blow completes the act.

The Romans want nails immediately,
as if they appear born in my hell pit;
almost magically with no skill involved.
What do they know of the value of the nail?—
rope is cheaper.

Besides, the pain of the nail doubles the anguish,
piercing naked skin of the hand and foot
to mount an innocent upon a cross.
They ask for four nails for their duty,
Yet they use only three. Thieves themselves.

I rest and eat at the twelfth hour,
and I see my results put to use.

Who is this man whose peace shines,
with the pierce of my nail?
Who would do this for me?

My eyes view my handiwork, and, ashamed,
I feel pain in my hands and feet.
I will become a farmer, a vintner.
The centurion slyly hides the fourth nail
in his cloak. For all to see.

R O P E   D A N C E R

Oppression grasps my heart tongue;
its hold shakes me weak.
I prayed for a King to set us free, and
yet, he preached only kindness.
I thirsted for swords to clash and sing
with smattering might, and
yet, he preached only forgiveness.
I hungered for power and wealth, and
yet, he preached only of love.

Those other doting fools did his bidding,
but I was the keeper of the sack,
the one to pay the bills,
the one to account for the coins,
the one who was the last to leave.

I resolved to have no more false hope;
I would play to the highest bidder
to sell my wares to the holies.
A mere kiss upon a cheek,
a soft toxin of identity,
and I would be victorious.
The price of thirty pieces of silver
would avenge his betrayal of me.

The torch-lit mob descended into the garden,
and I nudged his cheek with a kiss.
A piercing embrace on his soft skin.
His sad look punctured my heart,
and I felt very alone, yet very loved.
I ran to the temple to undo my wrong,
only to be cast aside, shunned.

A wrong must be righted, but how?
I kissed the wrong man; I kissed an innocent.
Now it is time for me to pay the final tariff.

I spy a coiled serpent of rope by the wall
and run to a field with a high tree;
its branched arms spread wide, welcoming.
With knot fastened about gnarled branch and neck,
I cry for forgiveness, for pity.
As my weight descends with cracking speed,
I jerk and twist and wriggle and spin
until my blood drips onto the cold clay
beneath me.

Before my eyes darken toward the heavens,
I see a surprising image—
I see him holding me gently,
my cloak tugged tight by his nailed hand,
and his eyes caress my soul
as he presses me to his heart.

R E L U C T A N C E

I hate to make decisions.
I can read the law, reach a verdict—
yet I hate to make decisions.

Now I am forced to go beyond the law.
I must find a way to silence a rebellion;
I must find a way to make peace.

Let the people make the decisions;
let the people have their way;
give them what they want, and
Let peace be had.

My wife gives me shudders;
she has visions.
She proclaims the future.
She bites my shoulder with prophecy,
and she throws me in turmoil.

What do I do with this Jew King?
He will walk my steps for sentence,
steps climbed by others who:
        begged for pardon,
        begged for forgiveness,
        begged for truth.

And I, the final judge must:
        execute a decision,
        execute a sentence,
        execute a hope . . . .

Yes, I must judge, must rule,
and I will do so, but

let me sleep if I am able.
Let me do right—
if I am able.

He walks the steps as planned,
a Man clothed in dusty robe,
a Man with conviction on His face,
a Man with peace in His eyes.
He walks to face me—
His gaze meets mine.

I know who is the victor, yet
I am in power.
I am he who will pass sentence;
I will exist with my decision.

As I glance at His brow,
I think of peace;
I am overcome with peace,
I feel forgiveness, and yet,
I have not passed sentence.

There must be another way.
My brain tricks quickly;
I ask the crowd, *What do you want?*
I beseech the mob, *What do you want?*
I implore the people, *Whom do you want to die?*
I cajole the masses, *Whom do you want to be free?*

If they offer the answer,
if they make the decision,
I will be free.
I can go safely home.

I ask again what they want, and
with all bellows aflame, they scream:
Give us Barabbas!
Give us Barabbas!
Done.

But my problem remains:
what do I do with this Jesus?
what do I do with this "Christ"?
what do I do with Him?
Barabbas' disposition was easy;
This gentle rogue is another matter.

And the mob gives me the verdict:
CRUCIFY HIM!
I beseech them, *But what has he done?*
CRUCIFY HIM!

I do their deafening will;
I wash my hands.

As He proceeds down the steps,
He stops at the third from the top, turns,
and looks at me. He smiles
a knowing glance, and utters: *I forgive you.*

With that, I dismiss myself; I turn away.
I must have some sustenance after this ordeal.
Some bread to cure the churning in my stomach,
a cup of wine to soothe my ills, but
I chew and drink hastily, and
I choke.

SIMON'S THOUGHTS

I

I work in the fields.
To you who do not know,
the work is not pleasant.
I travel on callused knees
and pick and scrape the
tiny weeds away from
sweet fruit.
And as I pick,
My hands cup inward,
twist the pain from the soil,
and as I attack those green serpents,
my knuckles scrape bare,
my blood nourishes the soil.
I do this each day and
each night I soak my hands
in water—
cool water to cleanse;
cool water to purify.

I question my laborious tasks—
Is this what I must do?
Is this my purpose in life?
To kneel and beg amidst the weeds—
To scour and pluck,
To throw, toss away the sin of the field?
I do not own the vineyard; that I know.
I merely bare my back here—
My tanned shoulders,
my burnt brow. My banged fingers remove
that which hurts and sucks away
the fruit.

Maybe someday these bronzed shoulders
and blood-dried hands will do
some real good. But of that,
I know not what.

I I

In the fields I hear the mumble
of others;
There is talk of a King
who is about to arrive,
who is about to come.

My friends in the field await
his majesty,
his force,
his voice.

Throughout their labors, they smile
and rejoice that the King will lift them—
above their pain,
above their torment,
above all that they do not know.

And for me, there is no King.
There is only the weed and the grape.
No more talk of this King.
No one can lift the pain in my body.
No one understands the hurt in my hands.
This King must be for others.
This King must not be for me.
For who am I?
I am the poorest of the poor;
I barely give my family the bread they need,
I cannot afford the wine
to quench the bread's thirst—
I merely breathe, for I must!
Ha!—I laugh at this King.
Will He give me bread?

Will He give me drink?
If He came into my House,
I would have nothing to offer.
Except my poor self.

I I I

On my way home,
I am stopped in the alley.
There is a parade on the main street.
I hear the voice of mayhem.
I move forward;
I inch to the roadway.
In front of me
I see what I have never seen before.
A man—shrouded in bloodied linen.
Thorns, digging deep into his brow like a crown;
a ragged cloak wrapped around a beaten body
and a cross draped over His right shoulder.
I ask: who is this poor Man?
What did He do?
What is He doing?
No crime is worth this pain, I think.
And then He falls.
The tricky, cobbled way,
the weight of the huge cross
makes him stumble onto the ground.
He is weak;
the pain oozes from His being.
The leaders of the parade know what to do.
They look to the crowds—
An eye catches mine.
You—come here.
I look away, pretending to see another.
The Roman hand grabs my collar and thrusts me
onto the cross.
You—help the Man with the cross.
Why me? I am slapped with the sword.
You—pick up His cross—help Him.

I fear for my life.
I position the crossbeam on top of my shoulder.
I begin to walk.
He is by my side.
He lifts some of the weight off my shoulders.
My mind wanders somewhere.
Why do I have to do this?
I've done no wrong. I've hurt no one.
Why are they crucifying me?
Who is this Man?
What did He do?
I slowly move forward. This journey seems endless.
I continue to ask myself:
Why am I here?

I V

So we carry the cross together—
Our shoulders push the crossbeam uphill.
The wood is heavy, yet
we trudge forward—
wherever that is—

I hear no sound; the jeering of the crowd
ends before it starts;
their words, their utterances are meaningless.

Our sandals strain at our arches—
this cross must be made of iron—
yet we move forward—
Who is this Man? Why am I here?

There is a pause—a woman
lunges from the crowd—she holds
forth a damp towel—she bathes
His face for comfort. Her tears
must have dampened the cloth—He
removes the veil; He is at peace—
How can He be at peace with so
much pain? How can He give peace
with so much pain?

We continue upward. I am
weak. My heart pounds
louder than the beat of the drum.
I twist my ankle on a cobblestone.

The cross falls on me.
He falls on me.

I cannot move.
His eyes pierce mine—
I must go on—
I cannot move—
He smiles:
You are a good servant—
I lie on the stones—the people
walk over me. He moves forward.

He has a journey to end;
I cannot be a part of it—
I lie in the street.
The stones press into my body,
and I cry that I cannot
move forward.
My shoulders are dented with blood,
my hands scraped bare by the
rough-hewn cross,
my sandals torn, my feet raw.

Dark clouds gather.
When I am able to kneel, I see afar;
past the trembling bodies
I see Him on a cross—and
I cry again, I cry to my Friend—and plead:
please come into
my house—I know I am healed.
Let me offer You my bread;
I will find the wine—then
I know I will be healed.

V

And now it is over.
I cannot ever forget this day.

This cross is heavy,
This cross is light.
The longer I carry this cross,
The lighter it becomes.
I think the longer I carry it,
It should become heavier—
but—it does not.
I don't understand; it is not heavy.
The longer I carry this weight,
the lighter it becomes.
How can this be?
It does not make sense.
It simply cannot be—yet
it is true.
The weight of the cross diminishes with time.
This defies what is known;
this defies reason;
this defies fact.
When I carry Christ's cross,
the weight is that of a feather.

But now I understand—
He carries the weight—
I only carry the cross.

VERONICA

No one knows me;
I, a mere lonely woman,
who cleans and cares the house.

I am a quiet woman;
I welcome no disturbance;
I treasure my aloneness.

Mob-bruised shouts draw me outside,
jeers and cheers resound amplified.
Spittle splashes Him.

Agony is present—
plodding of sandal spits sand
and stone.

I view the drama from afar;
my eyes comprehend not the play.
I move closer to follow
the path of the performance.

I cry with disgust and anger;
a splash of blood attacks my robe,
and I am weakened.
I feel hopeless and naked.

But now I see the performer;
He is scourged, tired, and weak.
Bloodied sweat and grime crease His face.
He stumbles close to the ground
under the weight of the wood.

He stops near me, to rest a moment;
His gasp for air is troubled.
I rush to His side and offer
my scarf to dry His face.

In the briefest moment, I wipe
His brow and offer comfort.
When I retrieve the cloth, I see
the gentlest visage, the calm
of his eyes, and His smile.

He returns on His journey, and
I on mine.
Only this time I am not alone,
I am not hopeless, for
I carry Him with me forever—
His countenance emblazoned not
only on my scarf, but on my heart.

VOICE OF EMBRACE

I remember, once, a friend
about to be stoned for adultery,
about to be shunned for sin.
Stones were gathered, placed pile-like,
Eagerness possessed the eyes of men.
The sentence was pronounced as
the droplets formed on the forehead,
twisted knuckle grasped any pebble.

But in an instant, He appeared.
He was calm; He was silent.
He was power, and He was robed in white.

He posed a question to the elders, then
drew it in the sand, quietly.
He looked up and asked:
Who of you is without sin? When you
answer truth, you may cast the first stone.
In shame, their eyes dropped to the earth;
they shuffled and dismissed themselves.

And then He raised my friend from the dust,
His piercing eye was pure, honest, and
He simply proclaimed—*Depart. Sin no more.*
And so she did.

From then on, I followed Him.
I followed His voice, His wisdom, His Purity.
He made me glow when He spoke;
He made me clean with His words.
He made me understand forgiveness.

And on that day, that Friday,
I thought my world had come to an end.
On that afternoon before the Sabbath,
the sentence had been pronounced, and
the parade had begun:

with a whipping at the pillory
with sharp thorns adorning His head
with the weight of a cross
with the jeers of the mob
with the pain of each step
with so much anguish
with the sight of His mother
with so many falls
with help from an unknown one
with the wiping of His brow
with His nailing to the cross
with His words to the thieves
with His final words to Heaven and
until His departure from the cross.

And I sobbed and I cried.
I touched His bloodied brow.
I kissed the blood from my fingers
and I was pure once again.
We cleansed Him, we wrapped Him,
we prepared Him for his tomb.

I slept not for days;
my life had ended.
I felt I was alone again;
my soul had departed—I was empty.

And on that third day,
I went to His tomb to pray, yet
upon my arrival, a Whiteness graced,
a Purity swelled within the tomb...
and the stone rolled flat on its back.

His Promise had become Truth.
His smile, His word, was with me.
And I smiled to myself in peace.
I was His friend, and He, mine;
and we will be together always,
we will be one, alone never again,
until we meet again.

BOOKENDS

I, Desmas, see my life float before me;
I see a time in the past in Egypt.
My cohort, Gesmas, spies a small caravan,
Moving through the desert unattended—
It is time to strike.

It is time to pillage and rob innocent souls.
As we approach on our steeds, I notice
A humble family of three choking forward.
They have nothing of value or want;
Their saddles and bags look empty.

I gaze at the mother with her child;
I look into the child's eyes.
They are poor with nothing to offer;
They run from Herod in fear.
I let them go; I set them free.

We move on, looking for others.
The desert is dry and painful,
the winds split the cheek; yet
I cannot remove His eye from my mind.
His image is upon me.

And in another time, years past,
I find myself wrapped in chains.
I am a convicted robber, a thief.
Gesmas and I face the same court.
Guilty. The sentence—crucifixion.

The time has come for death on a cross.
They lift us up, one with the other;

I, on the right; Gesmas on His left.
He is not one of us; He is pure.
The ropes burn my arms and feet.

I know death will be long and strained;
yet he wears a thorned crown, and
nails through his wrists and feet.
My God, what did this man do?
Why is His suffering so great?

The three of us groan in pain together.
Gesmas screams at him for salvation,
to save us if He is, indeed, a king.
I look to His eyes and see a child, and
I now know who He is, and I whimper.

Lord, forgive me, I say.
And He turns his chin upon His breast,
looks at me, those eyes so loving,
and says that I am with Him in Paradise.
Forever. He sets me free.

THE STONE-CUTTER

My hands are callused from hammer and chisel,
I have a callus upon a callus,
The stone chips and dust bite my fingers.
I have chip scars upon my cheek and brows,
I work for what is nothing.

I am now charged to build a burial home,
Joseph desires his permanent home.
He selected a cave-rock for his residence,
And I must hollow out the cave, and I must
Carve the sealing stone—no difficult task.

My hunched shoulders ache with pain,
My wrists begin to lose strength; yet
The chips of stone must fall before presence becomes
A final resting place, a place for comfort,
A place where the soul can rest.

But today I am given an order for completion
Within a day, and the sealing stone must be done also.
Joseph gives up his resting place for another;
One whom I am told is the greatest of teachers,
One whom I am told is Jesus, the Savior.

I know nothing of a savior; I only know of callus.
I know only of sweat and stone and completion, but
An order is an order, and the sealing stone must be done.
The stone must seal perfectly—no seams, just tightness.
The stone seam must be perfect; unopened forever.

I chisel and sand late into the evening,
Time is forever, I am told, and I finish my task.

Now for sleep, for my body aches with pain,
My task is complete, and I am proud of my work.
The tomb is now ready to receive Whomever.

I sleep in the bushes, too tired to return home;
Yet when I awake in the late afternoon, I can only gasp.
They bring the body of this Savior to my tomb;
He is bloodied in His shroud, yet he looks at peace.
He is placed in the tomb, gently, forever.

I am ordered to seal the opening;
I do so, and laboriously roll the stone to the orifice.
I peek inside for a final look, only peace and silence.
The stone creaks into place, and I seal with limestone.
Nothing can break this seal, no human strength can undo.

Three days later, I am summoned to the tomb,
The women show me the rolled-away stone, and I
Am amazed. I humble myself before them, but
They say my work is perfect, and I know no shame.
For His power is above all earthly strength.

And to this day, I marvel at His power,
And I question His Being, and I ponder my own soul.
I only wish I could have known Him,
I only pray that He knows me, and that He has forgiven me
For building his temporary tomb. Amen.

ON THOMAS'S TERMS

I am a free thinker—
I am one of doubt of all—
I take no terms or understanding quickly—
I must be shown and proven to—
for I am Thomas.

I was with Jesus at the house
where Lazarus lived.
I was with Jesus at the tomb
where Lazarus lay.
I heard the command
for Lazarus to come forward.
I witnessed his arousal,
and I believed.

Yet now I am alone in fear.
My brothers meet behind closed doors,
with limited light.
They are braver than I,
with fearless strength,
they huddle in faith.

I am told of a visit to them
when I was not there.
I crouch in silence and darkness.
Jesus was there,
and I was absent.

Another time comes forward;
I am with my brothers again.
They tell me of the visit, of the awe:
He stood before us,

He told of His Love for us,
He gave us our direction,
He brought comfort to us;
and I angrily spit out:
i was not here,
i did not see,
i did not hear, and
i did not witness!

My brothers pull back and sigh;
I continue:
i must see the holes of the nails,
i must plunge my fingers there,
i must puncture again His side,
i must sense His presence.

And then, He appears through closed doors.
He glances among us and
His presence beams like a diamond rainbow.
I can only bow my head;
I cannot look; I cannot see.

He walks to me and opens His palms.
Thomas, do what you must—
Place your fingers in the nail post,
Place your hand in My pierced side.
Do what you must.

And I, choking upon my tears, cannot touch.
I lie prostrate before Him, begging:
for forgiveness,
for understanding,
for faith,
for His love.

And He extends not my agony.
He pulls me up by my shoulders,
looks me in the eye, and
pronounces: *BELIEVE.*

I fall again to the ground, and
once again He rescues me upward.
His Soul says to me:
You believe because you can see.
Blessed are those who have not seen,
and yet believe.

I tumble a third time to my knees before Him—
Peace is mine.

JUSTUS

I lost to the lot;
I was second of two
to be the twelfth of twelve,
to fill the void
of death-absent Judas.

We prayed in dim-lit darkness.
The upper room clothed our fear
and offered its protection.
A single candle provided shadows
to balance our prayer.

As morning neared, we slid out
one by one into the coolness.
I was alone wrapped in thought:
what to do, where to go.
I decided to move forward.

I could not be one of the twelve,
but I could be a disciple of love.
I could speak the word of Jesus;
I could speak of His love;
I would do so with His passion.

I know in my heart,
I did not lose—I won.
My words gave me freedom,
My words gave others peace;
And I sing with glee in my heart.

II

CHARTRES

Live in Christ's diamond, and
Let its sharp brilliant tongue
Touch your eye, your heart.
Let its angles and angels of light
Pierce your being with warmth.
Let its blinding blue,
Let its scarlet pain,
Let its earthly greens,
Let its golden suns,
Fragment your actuality.
Breathe the soul of this house:
Drink deeply the depth of power,
Ponder the wisdom of the window,
Circle the labyrinth quietly,
Each smoothed stone, a memory,
An empty presence of those past, and
Leave your existence in the limestone,
Only to return forever.

S A I N T   M A R T I N

A cold and bitter night swipes at my face,
but I must check my troops,
the men must see that their leader
is with them, they need to know I am here.

I curse this foul night!
I was warm by my fire,
yet the chill in my heart is nothing
compared with the cold of loneliness—
the bared shoulder,
the unclothed foot remembers
nothing of the warmth
of another time
of another moment.

My men are sheltered for the night,
for the moment;
I can return to my safety.
Ah, I am glad this tribute is paid
for I know they will serve me
well tomorrow.

When I turn into the alley, my horse
brushes the wall, my armor scrapes
and sparks there;
the cobbled stone blocks rhythm,
and my eye captures a huddle
in the corner.

A half-naked man—a chill abounds
His being.
He raises his hand—I pause.

His eyes pierce mine;
No words are spoken.
His plea grasps me about the throat.

He does not speak—
darkness swallows the alley.
Yet a light glimmers, flickers around
His eyes;
and I grasp my sword,
slice my scarlet cloak,
lean from my horse, and
offer a tatter of cloth
to my Beggar.
He grasps it quickly,
wraps it, like a shroud,
and smiles.

Blackness becomes warmth.
When I look up—the darkness
is absent; there is only light,
but
He is gone—
and now, I know what I
must do.

A SIMPLE HYMN

I walk in the fields of the Lord.
My heart sings to the flowers,
my heart sings to the sun.
My heart sings to Him
Who makes my field His pasture.

GARDEN THOUGHTS

I work alone in my garden;
I am alone with my thoughts.

Dear God,
Your garden is perfection,
and I:

Thank You
for light-encircling my soul.

Thank You
for wind-kissing my cheek.

Thank You
for color-brightening my day.

Thank You
for sun-warming my heart.

Thank You
for water-cleansing my being.

Thank You
for your Son saving me forever.

I work alone in my garden;
I am alone with my thoughts—
well, almost alone.

LORD, LET IT BE

Lord, let it be
peace;
Lord, let it be
happiness.

Please pass gray clouds away,
let sunlight bloom,
make the sky blue.

Lord, let it be
peace;
Lord, let it be
happiness.

Please carry my mother to You;
rest her gently in Your arms,
as she has done so often for me.

Lord, let it be
peace;
Lord, let it be
happiness.

Please accept my prayer for her,
one sweet kiss upon her cheek,
to let her come home.

Lord, let it be peace;
Lord, let it be joy!
Lord, let it be.

NEVER ALONE

Oh, Lord Jesus:
thank You for today,
thank You for the sun,
blue sky and breeze that
swirls within my soul;
for it is Your breath
that moves me forward.

Thank You for You; for gifts
so simple, so pure, so peaceful
that surround and protect me.

Yes, You and I together share:
a calming bond,
a loving touch;
a welcoming embrace.

Without You
I am alone.

RECONCILIATION

Reconciliation is not
  a Saturday in the box,
  a one-time visit before Christmas,
  a one-time visit before Easter.

Reconciliation is today
  an everyday prayer;
  an everyday examination
  of what was and what will be.

Reconciliation is the power
  to do better, to make amends,
  to purify the conscience,
  to move forward.

Reconciliation is a Thank You,
Thank You to God, to Jesus.
To sin is human—
To pardon is God's will.

The Holy Spirit dances on our shoulders,
  only to guide us to purity;
  only to open our souls,
  only to make us clean.

Peace begins with a Thank You,
and a humble *I am sorry*—
What more is there to be asked?

S I L E N T   P R A Y E R

(Found in a French church)

Lord, I do not know how to pray, but
I have come here to burn a candle.
I admit that it is very little…

It is nothing, really... but it is a sign.
It is the sign that I want to stay
for a little while, in silence, near You.

YES

Yes, God did cry when Jesus died;
How could He not?
To see Your loved one hurt so much,
To feel His pain, Your pain.
Jesus doing this for You—
Jesus knowing; Your knowing,
Jesus dying this death for all:
Jesus expiring for the future—
And all in the name of freedom;
All in the name of hope; and
All in the name of memory—
That is all that is asked.

His tears filled oceans,
His tears soaked up desert sands,
His tears froze ice-capped mountains;
His tears are forever present; just
Listen to the rains, to the snows.

Yes, God did cry when Jesus died;
Only listen to His voice in the winds....
And the rains, for
He cries every day—
For us.

SOMETIMES

Jesus leaves me alone, and that is good;
I love him even more.

Solitude can be peaceful or painful;
Depends on where you are.
Working through pain promotes peace, and
Isolation blankets pain, providing warmth.

Jesus is the blanket, and that is good;
I love him even more.

Stumbling within peace makes calm;
Depends on where you are.
All edges wrap the warmth or heart, and
Peace comforts the soul

Jesus is the peace and that is good;
I love him even more.

When we accept aloneness and isolation,
We must remember we are not alone,
Now, that is a good friend, and
Sometimes he is always there.

THE CYRENEAN PRAYER

Oh Lord, give me strength
        to help those in need; please:

Grant me the will to bend down
        and hold a child in distress;

Send me the Grace
        to caress a grieving soul;

Provide me the patience to endure
        insult and hateful words;

Award me the desire to carry
        the crosses of others;

Hand me Your peace to instill
        in others a faith so pure;

Cause me, oh Lord, to live your life
        so others, too, will carry your cross.

ABOUT THE AUTHOR

Richard Martin Lukesh, a retired educator, lives in West Milford, New Jersey, with his wife, Christine, his dog, Satchel, and two cats, Autumn and Clover. Their son, Matt, is co-owner of Seppuku Tattoo, a tattoo studio and art gallery in Savannah, Georgia, and their daughter, Sarah, an underwriter for a major insurance company, resides in upstate New York. Richard has been writing practically all his life, and *The Cyrenean Prayers,* his first book of poetry, is a work ten years in the making. He is currently working on a second book entitled *Boiled Toast and Other Delicacies.* An avid traveler, Richard has journeyed throughout Europe and Asia; he considers Paris his second home. The poet is a graduate of King's College, Wilkes-Barre, Pennsylvania, studied at Wroxton College in England, and earned two graduate degrees at Fairleigh Dickinson University, Teaneck, New Jersey.

Photo courtesy of Sarah Lukesh

2445711

Made in the USA